Tech Ethics:

Navigating the Moral Dilemmas of the Digital Age

By

Eugenia C. Gauvin

TABLE OF CONTENTS

CHAPTER IX

CHAPTER X

CHAPTER I
Introduction

A. Importance of technology ethics in the digital age

In today's digital age, where technology permeates every aspect of our lives, the importance of technology ethics cannot be overstated. As we become increasingly reliant on digital tools and platforms, we find ourselves confronted with a myriad of moral dilemmas that demand our attention and thoughtful consideration. The decisions we make in the realm of technology have far-reaching consequences that can impact individuals, societies, and even the future of humanity.

Technology ethics, also known as tech ethics, involves the study and application of ethical principles to the development, deployment, and use of technology. It encompasses a broad range of issues, including privacy, data protection, artificial intelligence, automation, bias, discrimination, cybersecurity, and the ethical responsibilities of tech companies. The rapid pace of technological advancement often outstrips our ability to fully comprehend the ethical implications of these innovations, making it crucial for us to navigate this complex landscape with care and deliberation.

One of the primary reasons why technology ethics has gained immense significance is the immense power that technology wields in shaping our lives. From social media algorithms influencing our preferences and beliefs to AI-powered systems making decisions that affect our access to opportunities, technology has the potential to greatly impact our well-being, values, and fundamental rights. Without a solid ethical foundation, the unchecked use of technology can lead to unintended consequences and moral quandaries.

Furthermore, technology has the capacity to amplify existing inequalities and create new ones. Issues such as privacy breaches, algorithmic bias, and digital divide underscore the urgency of addressing ethical concerns in the digital age. If we fail to adequately address these challenges, we risk perpetuating systemic biases, compromising individual autonomy, and exacerbating social injustices.

Technology ethics also plays a crucial role in building trust and fostering responsible innovation. As the public becomes more aware of the potential harms that can arise from the misuse of technology, there is a growing demand for ethical considerations to be integrated into the design and implementation of technological solutions. By incorporating ethical frameworks, we can ensure that technology serves the greater good, respects human rights, and promotes fairness and justice.

In conclusion, the importance of technology ethics in the digital age cannot be emphasized enough. It is not enough to simply marvel at the wonders of technology; we must also critically examine its ethical dimensions. By proactively addressing the moral dilemmas that arise in this digital era, we can steer technology towards a more ethical path, one that aligns with our values, safeguards our rights, and promotes the well-being of individuals and societies as a whole.

B. Definition of technology ethics

Technology ethics, also known as tech ethics or digital ethics, refers to the branch of ethics that deals with the moral principles, values, and guidelines governing the development, deployment, and use of technology in the digital age. It is a multidisciplinary field that combines elements of philosophy, sociology, psychology, law, and computer science to address the ethical implications of technological advancements.

At its core, technology ethics seeks to examine the impact of technology on individuals, societies, and the environment, and to guide responsible decision-making in the realm of technology. It recognizes that technological innovations have profound consequences, both intended and unintended, and that these consequences must be carefully evaluated from an ethical standpoint.

The field of technology ethics encompasses a wide range of issues and dilemmas. It explores questions related to privacy and data protection, as well as the ethical considerations surrounding the collection, storage, and use of personal information in the digital realm. It also delves into the ethical implications of artificial intelligence and automation, addressing concerns such as bias, discrimination, and the potential loss of human autonomy.

Moreover, technology ethics examines the ethical responsibilities of tech companies and the role they play in shaping society. It scrutinizes issues such as corporate social responsibility, fair business practices, and the impact of technology on employment and economic inequality. Additionally, it explores the ethical dimensions of internet and digital media, including topics such as freedom of speech, online harassment, and the spread of disinformation.

In essence, technology ethics provides a framework for evaluating the moral dimensions of technological advancements. It helps us navigate the complex terrain of the digital age by encouraging critical thinking, fostering awareness of potential harms, and promoting ethical decision-making. By examining the ethical implications of technology, we can strive to ensure that technological progress aligns with our values, respects human rights, and contributes to the betterment of society.

It is important to note that technology ethics is an evolving field, as new technologies and their associated ethical challenges continue to emerge. As our reliance on technology deepens, so does the need for ongoing discussions, debates, and ethical frameworks to guide our actions. By engaging in these conversations and actively considering the ethical dimensions of technology, we can collectively shape a future that harnesses the power of technology while upholding our shared moral principles and ideals.

C. Overview of the moral dilemmas faced in the digital age

The digital age has ushered in a host of transformative technologies that have revolutionized the way we live, work, and interact. However, alongside these remarkable advancements, we find ourselves confronted with a multitude of moral dilemmas that demand our attention and contemplation. This section provides an overview of the key moral dilemmas faced in the digital age, shedding light on the complex ethical landscape that technology presents.

One of the foremost moral dilemmas revolves around privacy and data ethics. With the vast amount of personal information being collected, stored, and analyzed by various entities, questions arise regarding the protection of individuals' privacy rights. Balancing the benefits of data-driven technologies with the potential risks of surveillance, data breaches, and the commodification of personal information is a significant challenge in the digital age.

Artificial intelligence (AI) and automation present another ethical frontier. As AI systems become increasingly sophisticated, they are making decisions that have profound implications for individuals and society. The issue of bias in algorithms, for instance, raises concerns about discrimination and fairness in areas such as hiring, lending, and criminal justice. Striking a balance between the power of AI and the preservation of human values and rights is a pressing moral dilemma.

The prevalence of online platforms and social media has given rise to questions of digital media ethics. The spread of fake news, online harassment, and the manipulation of public opinion challenge our notions of freedom of speech, accountability, and the responsible use of technology. The ethical responsibilities of both users and platforms in curating and disseminating information in a manner that upholds truth, transparency, and the well-being of individuals and societies are under scrutiny.

Moreover, the digital age has brought attention to issues of cybersecurity and ethical hacking. The increasing sophistication of cyber threats necessitates robust security measures, but at the same time, striking a balance between security and personal privacy is crucial. Ethical hacking, with its aim to uncover vulnerabilities and protect against malicious actors, raises questions about the ethical boundaries of accessing and manipulating systems in the name of security.

Additionally, questions surrounding the ethical responsibilities of technology companies loom large. The immense power and influence of tech giants raise concerns about their impact on democracy, labor rights, and economic equality. Corporate social responsibility, fair business practices, and the ethical design and deployment of technology are all part of the moral dilemmas faced in the digital age.

These are just a few examples of the complex moral dilemmas that technology presents. As the digital landscape continues to evolve, so too will the ethical challenges we encounter. Navigating these dilemmas requires thoughtful consideration, interdisciplinary collaboration, and an ongoing commitment to ensuring that our technological advancements align with our moral values and contribute positively to the well-being of individuals and society as a whole.

CHAPTER II
The Impact of Technology on Society

A. Positive effects of technology

The impact of technology on society in the digital age has been profound and far-reaching, bringing about numerous positive effects that have transformed the way we live, work, and connect with one another. This section explores some of the key positive impacts of technology on society, highlighting the advancements that have enriched our lives.

One of the most significant positive effects of technology is the increased accessibility and availability of information. The internet has revolutionized the way we seek and obtain knowledge, enabling us to access a vast array of information at our fingertips. This has democratized education, allowing individuals from all walks of life to pursue learning and gain new skills. It has also facilitated the dissemination of information, empowering people to stay informed about global events, participate in civic discourse, and engage with diverse perspectives.

Technology has also revolutionized communication, breaking down geographical barriers and connecting people across the globe. The advent of social media, messaging apps, and video conferencing platforms has facilitated instant and seamless communication, enabling individuals, families, and communities to stay connected regardless of physical distance. This has fostered meaningful relationships, promoted cultural exchange, and enhanced collaboration on a global scale.

In the realm of healthcare, technology has played a transformative role in improving patient care, diagnosis, and treatment. From electronic health records and telemedicine to medical imaging and precision medicine, technology has enhanced the efficiency and accuracy of healthcare delivery. It has empowered patients to take control of their health through wearable devices and health-tracking apps, promoting preventive care and personalized medicine.

Moreover, technology has revolutionized various industries, driving economic growth and creating new opportunities. Automation and digitalization have increased productivity and efficiency in sectors such as manufacturing, logistics, and agriculture. This has led to advancements in production processes, reduced costs, and enhanced the quality of goods and services. Technology has also facilitated the rise of innovative startups and entrepreneurship, fostering economic dynamism and job creation.

Another positive impact of technology on society is its ability to promote social activism and civic engagement. Social media platforms have become powerful tools for organizing grassroots movements, raising awareness about social issues, and mobilizing collective action. They have given marginalized voices a platform to be heard, facilitating social change and holding institutions accountable. Technology has also enabled philanthropic endeavors, making it easier for individuals to support causes and contribute to positive societal impact.

In conclusion, technology has brought about numerous positive effects on society in the digital age. From increased access to information and enhanced communication to advancements in healthcare, economic growth, and social activism, technology has transformed our lives in remarkable ways. It is important to acknowledge and harness these positive impacts while also addressing the ethical challenges and potential negative consequences to ensure that technology continues to serve as a force for good and benefit all members of society.

B. Negative effects of technology

While technology has undoubtedly brought about significant advancements and positive impacts on society, it is important to recognize and address the negative effects that accompany these technological developments. This section delves into some of the key negative effects of technology on society, shedding light on the challenges and concerns that arise in the digital age.

One of the prominent negative effects of technology is the erosion of privacy. With the proliferation of digital devices, social media platforms, and online services, individuals' personal information has become increasingly vulnerable to breaches and unauthorized access. The collection and utilization of personal data by corporations and governments have raised concerns about surveillance, data mining, and the potential misuse of sensitive information. The erosion of privacy jeopardizes individuals' autonomy and can lead to discrimination, manipulation, and the violation of fundamental rights.

Technology has also contributed to a sedentary lifestyle and decreased physical activity. With the rise of screens and sedentary entertainment, such as video games and streaming services, people are spending more time indoors and leading increasingly sedentary lives. This has detrimental effects on physical and mental health, contributing to issues such as obesity, decreased fitness levels, and social isolation.

Moreover, the rapid pace of technological advancements has given rise to concerns about job displacement and economic inequality. Automation and artificial intelligence have the potential to replace human labor in various sectors, leading to job losses and a shifting employment landscape. This has resulted in increased economic disparities, as individuals with the necessary skills and access to resources benefit more from the digital economy, while others are left behind. The digital divide exacerbates existing inequalities, with marginalized communities often lacking access to the opportunities and benefits that technology offers.

Technology has also had an impact on mental well-being, giving rise to issues such as information overload, digital addiction, and cyberbullying. The constant connectivity and exposure to social media can lead to feelings of anxiety, stress, and decreased self-esteem. The pressure to maintain an idealized online persona and the negative interactions that can occur in digital spaces contribute to mental health challenges, particularly among younger generations.

In addition, technology has facilitated the spread of misinformation and the manipulation of public opinion. The ease of sharing information on social media platforms has given rise to the dissemination of fake news, conspiracy theories, and propaganda. This not only undermines the trust in reliable sources of information but also poses a threat to democratic processes and societal cohesion.

It is crucial to acknowledge these negative effects of technology to effectively address the ethical dilemmas they present. By recognizing the challenges associated with privacy, physical and mental health, employment, inequality, and information integrity, we can work towards finding solutions that mitigate these negative impacts. Striking a balance between technological advancements and the well-being of individuals and society is essential to ensure that technology continues to serve as a force for positive change.

C. Ethical implications of technological advancements

Technological advancements have revolutionized society, bringing about significant changes that have both positive and negative implications. In this section, we delve into the ethical implications of these technological advancements, highlighting the complex ethical landscape that emerges in the digital age.

One of the primary ethical implications is the issue of privacy and data protection. The widespread collection, storage, and utilization of personal data raise concerns about the safeguarding of individual privacy rights. The ethical dilemma lies in striking a balance between the benefits of data-driven technologies, such as personalized services and targeted advertising, and the potential risks of surveillance, data breaches, and the commodification of personal information. Addressing the ethical implications of data ethics requires robust regulations, transparency, informed consent, and clear accountability mechanisms.

Artificial intelligence (AI) presents another significant ethical frontier. The increasing capabilities of AI systems raise concerns about transparency, accountability, and potential biases. AI algorithms can perpetuate existing social biases and discrimination, impacting areas such as hiring, lending, and criminal justice. Ensuring fairness, equity, and accountability in AI decision-making is crucial to prevent discriminatory outcomes and uphold ethical principles.

Furthermore, technological advancements bring about ethical considerations related to automation and the future of work. Automation has the potential to replace human labor in various sectors, leading to job displacement and economic inequality. The ethical dilemma lies in finding ways to address these societal impacts, ensuring the equitable distribution of benefits and providing avenues for reskilling and upskilling. Striking a balance between efficiency and human well-being is paramount in shaping the future of work.

Another ethical implication is the impact of technology on social relationships and well-being. The rise of social media and digital connectivity has transformed the way we interact and communicate. However, it also raises concerns about social isolation, addiction, and the erosion of authentic human connection. Balancing the benefits of digital connectivity with the need for meaningful face-to-face interactions and well-being is a crucial ethical consideration.

The ethical implications of technology extend to areas such as environmental sustainability and resource consumption. The rapid growth of technology and the digital economy contribute to the increasing demand for energy and resources. Minimizing the environmental footprint of technology, promoting sustainable practices, and addressing issues like electronic waste management are ethical imperatives for a sustainable future.

Moreover, technology presents ethical challenges concerning accountability and responsibility. The actions of tech companies, their influence on public discourse, and their responsibility in addressing issues such as misinformation, hate speech, and algorithmic biases raise ethical questions about corporate accountability and the societal impact of technological choices. Promoting transparency, corporate social responsibility, and ethical design principles are essential in addressing these concerns.

In conclusion, the ethical implications of technological advancements in society are multifaceted and require careful consideration. Privacy, AI ethics, automation and employment, social well-being, sustainability, and corporate responsibility are just a few of the ethical dimensions that arise in the digital age. By actively engaging in ethical discussions, fostering interdisciplinary collaboration, and establishing robust ethical frameworks, we can ensure that technology serves as a tool for positive change while upholding fundamental values and principles.

CHAPTER III
Ethical Frameworks for the Digital Age

A. Utilitarianism and its application in technology ethics

Utilitarianism, a consequentialist ethical framework, holds that the moral worth of an action is determined by its overall consequences and the maximization of overall happiness or well-being. In the context of technology ethics, utilitarianism provides a valuable perspective for evaluating the ethical implications of technological advancements and guiding decision-making.

Utilitarianism in technology ethics emphasizes the importance of considering the overall societal benefits and harms that arise from the development, deployment, and use of technology. It encourages the assessment of the positive and negative consequences on various stakeholders, including individuals, communities, and society as a whole.

One application of utilitarianism in technology ethics involves evaluating the impact of technological innovations on human well-being and quality of life.

Utilitarians consider how technology can enhance people's lives, improve access to resources and opportunities, and promote overall happiness. For example, the development of medical technologies that enable more accurate diagnoses and better treatments can lead to improved health outcomes and increased well-being for individuals and communities.

Utilitarianism also helps address issues of resource allocation and prioritization in technology development. By considering the greatest overall good, utilitarians can guide decisions regarding the allocation of resources towards technologies that have the potential to maximize benefits and mitigate harms. This may involve prioritizing technologies that address pressing societal challenges, such as clean energy or accessible education, based on their potential positive impact.

Another aspect where utilitarianism is applied in technology ethics is in assessing the social and economic impacts of technology. Utilitarians consider how technology affects the distribution of resources, economic inequality, and social well-being. They strive to ensure that technological advancements do not disproportionately benefit certain groups or perpetuate existing disparities. Utilitarians may advocate for policies and interventions that promote fairness, inclusivity, and social justice in the development and deployment of technology.

However, utilitarianism is not without its limitations in the realm of technology ethics. One challenge is the difficulty of accurately predicting and measuring the long-term consequences of technological advancements. The complexity of technology's impact on society, including unintended consequences and unforeseen risks, poses challenges for utilitarian analysis.

Additionally, utilitarianism may raise concerns about individual rights and the potential for sacrificing the well-being of a few for the greater good. Critics argue that utilitarianism can overlook the importance of protecting individual autonomy, privacy, and other fundamental rights in the pursuit of overall happiness.

Overall, utilitarianism offers a valuable ethical framework for technology ethics by emphasizing the examination of overall consequences and the maximization of well-being. By considering the potential benefits and harms of technology on various stakeholders and striving for the greatest overall good, utilitarianism can guide ethical decision-making and contribute to the responsible development and use of technology in the digital age.

B. Deontological ethics and its relevance in the digital age

Deontological ethics, often associated with philosophers like Immanuel Kant, focuses on the inherent moral principles and duties that guide human actions, regardless of their consequences. In the digital age, deontological ethics plays a crucial role in guiding ethical decision-making and addressing the complex moral dilemmas posed by technological advancements.

One key aspect of deontological ethics is its emphasis on moral duties and rights. Deontologists argue that individuals and institutions have certain moral obligations and responsibilities that should be upheld, regardless of the potential benefits or harms that may result. In the digital age, this framework helps address ethical considerations related to privacy, consent, transparency, and individual autonomy.

Deontological ethics is particularly relevant in the context of privacy and data ethics. It recognizes the inherent value of personal privacy and asserts that individuals have a fundamental right to control their personal information. From a deontological perspective, organizations and institutions have a duty to respect this right and protect individuals' privacy, even if doing so may limit potential benefits or data-driven insights.

Another area where deontological ethics is relevant in the digital age is in addressing issues of transparency and accountability. Deontologists argue that individuals and organizations have a moral duty to act with honesty, integrity, and transparency, especially in the context of technology development and use. This framework calls for clear rules, consent mechanisms, and accountability measures to ensure that individuals and communities can make informed decisions and hold responsible parties accountable.

Moreover, deontological ethics underscores the importance of individual autonomy and informed consent in the digital realm. It recognizes that individuals should have the freedom to make autonomous choices about the use and sharing of their personal information. This framework provides a basis for ethical considerations related to informed consent, user control, and the ethical design of user interfaces, ensuring that individuals are not coerced or manipulated into giving away their personal information or participating in activities that violate their autonomy.

Furthermore, deontological ethics guides discussions surrounding fairness and justice in the digital age. It emphasizes the equal moral worth of all individuals and asserts that fairness and justice should be upheld in the development and deployment of technology. This framework raises questions about issues such as algorithmic bias, discrimination, and the equitable distribution of the benefits and burdens of technological advancements. It calls for ethical considerations to ensure that technology does not perpetuate social injustices or create new forms of inequality.

While deontological ethics provides valuable insights in addressing ethical challenges in the digital age, it also has limitations. Critics argue that deontological principles can be rigid and may not adequately consider the consequences of actions. The balance between respecting individual rights and the potential benefits of technology may require thoughtful consideration and ethical trade-offs.

In conclusion, deontological ethics offers a relevant and valuable framework for addressing ethical considerations in the digital age. Its focus on moral duties, rights, transparency, accountability, and individual autonomy provides guidance in navigating complex moral dilemmas posed by technological advancements. By upholding moral principles and considering the inherent value of individual rights and autonomy, deontological ethics contributes to the responsible development, deployment, and use of technology in the digital age.

C. Virtue ethics and its role in guiding ethical decisions in technology

Virtue ethics, rooted in the works of ancient philosophers such as Aristotle, emphasizes the development of virtuous character traits and ethical behavior. In the digital age, virtue ethics plays a vital role in guiding ethical decisions and addressing the complex moral challenges arising from technological advancements.

Virtue ethics focuses on cultivating virtuous qualities and habits in individuals and organizations. It places importance on ethical virtues such as honesty, integrity, empathy, fairness, and respect for others. In the context of technology, virtue ethics calls for the development of virtuous character traits that guide ethical decision-making and promote responsible behavior.

One of the key aspects of virtue ethics in the digital age is fostering ethical leadership and professional responsibility. It encourages individuals working in technology-related fields to develop virtuous qualities such as integrity, accountability, and a commitment to ethical conduct. Ethical leaders in technology companies can set a positive example, promote responsible practices, and prioritize the well-being of individuals and society.

Virtue ethics also plays a crucial role in addressing issues of digital citizenship and responsible use of technology. It emphasizes the development of virtues such as digital empathy, digital literacy, and digital integrity. Practicing digital empathy involves understanding the impact of our actions online and considering the well-being of others in digital interactions. Digital literacy encompasses the ability to critically evaluate and navigate digital information while upholding ethical standards. Digital integrity involves behaving ethically and responsibly in the digital realm, including respecting others' privacy, refraining from cyberbullying, and avoiding the spread of misinformation.

Furthermore, virtue ethics guides ethical considerations related to the design and deployment of technology. It promotes the development of virtuous qualities in technologists, encouraging them to prioritize human values, well-being, and inclusivity in their work. Virtue ethics calls for technology to be designed in a manner that reflects ethical virtues, such as fairness, transparency, and the promotion of human flourishing. It encourages the development of technologies that empower individuals, foster meaningful connections, and enhance human capabilities.

Another aspect where virtue ethics is relevant in the digital age is in addressing the impact of technology on well-being and the balance between the digital and offline lives. Virtue ethics encourages individuals to cultivate virtues such as self-control, moderation, and mindfulness in their use of technology. It calls for individuals to reflect on their values, set healthy boundaries, and make intentional choices that promote personal well-being and the well-being of others.

While virtue ethics offers valuable insights, it also has limitations. Critics argue that it may lack clear guidelines and can be subjective in determining virtuous behavior. The application of virtue ethics may require ongoing reflection, dialogue, and the development of shared ethical norms within communities and organizations.

In conclusion, virtue ethics provides a valuable framework for guiding ethical decisions and promoting responsible behavior in the digital age. By focusing on the development of virtuous character traits, virtue ethics encourages individuals, leaders, and organizations to prioritize ethical values, foster digital citizenship, and design technologies that align with human well-being and flourishing. By cultivating virtuous qualities, we can navigate the ethical challenges posed by technological advancements and contribute to a more ethical and responsible digital society.

CHAPTER IV
Privacy and Data Ethics

A. Importance of privacy in the digital age

In the digital age, where technology has become deeply integrated into our lives, the importance of privacy has taken on a whole new dimension. Privacy is a fundamental human right that allows individuals to maintain control over their personal information and protect their autonomy, dignity, and freedom.

Privacy in the digital age is crucial for several reasons. Firstly, it enables individuals to have a sense of autonomy and control over their personal lives. It allows people to make choices about what information they share, with whom, and under what circumstances. Privacy empowers individuals to create boundaries, maintain a sense of personal space, and express themselves without fear of unnecessary scrutiny or judgment.

Secondly, privacy safeguards personal security and protects individuals from potential harm. The digital age presents numerous risks, such as identity theft, online fraud, stalking, and surveillance. Privacy measures, such as secure data encryption and strict access controls, play a vital role in safeguarding sensitive personal information and mitigating these risks. They help build trust and confidence in digital platforms and services, fostering a safe and secure online environment.

Moreover, privacy is closely tied to the notion of trust and the integrity of our relationships, both online and offline. When individuals have confidence that their personal information will be handled responsibly and respectfully, they are more likely to engage in open and honest communication, participate in online communities, and freely express their thoughts and opinions. Privacy nurtures an environment where individuals feel safe to explore, learn, and connect with others without fear of judgment or reprisal.

Privacy also plays a crucial role in preserving democratic values and civil liberties. In an increasingly interconnected world, where digital footprints are constantly being created and analyzed, privacy ensures that individuals can freely engage in political discourse, express dissenting views, and exercise their right to privacy. Privacy protects individuals from undue surveillance, censorship, and the chilling effect that surveillance can have on free speech and personal expression.

Furthermore, privacy is essential for fostering innovation and creativity. When individuals have confidence that their personal information will be protected, they are more likely to engage in online activities, share innovative ideas, and contribute to the development of new technologies and services. Privacy encourages a dynamic and vibrant digital ecosystem where individuals can freely explore, experiment, and collaborate without fear of undue scrutiny or exploitation.

In conclusion, privacy holds immense importance in the digital age. It is a fundamental right that protects individual autonomy, security, and well-being. Privacy fosters trust, enables freedom of expression, preserves civil liberties, and promotes innovation. As technology continues to advance, it is essential that privacy remains a cornerstone of ethical considerations, guiding the responsible use of personal data and ensuring that individuals' privacy rights are respected and upheld.

B. Ethical considerations in data collection and surveillance

Ethical considerations in data collection and surveillance have become increasingly important in the digital age. As technology allows for the collection, analysis, and storage of vast amounts of personal data, it is essential to address the ethical implications of these practices to protect individuals' privacy, autonomy, and fundamental rights.

One of the primary ethical considerations is the principle of informed consent. Individuals should have the right to know how their data is being collected, used, and shared. Organizations and service providers have an ethical responsibility to be transparent about their data practices and obtain meaningful consent from individuals before collecting their personal information. This requires clear communication, understandable terms and conditions, and empowering individuals to make informed choices about the use of their data.

Another important ethical consideration is data minimization. Organizations should only collect and retain the minimum amount of data necessary to fulfill the intended purpose. This principle reduces the risk of unauthorized access, data breaches, and the potential misuse of personal information. By adopting a data minimization approach, organizations demonstrate a commitment to respecting individuals' privacy and minimizing potential harm.

Data accuracy and integrity are additional ethical considerations. Organizations have an ethical duty to ensure that the data they collect and use is accurate, up to date, and reliable. Inaccurate or misleading data can lead to incorrect assumptions, biased decision-making, and unjust outcomes. Responsible data practices involve implementing appropriate measures to maintain data accuracy, such as regular data verification and validation processes.

Moreover, privacy by design is an ethical principle that calls for privacy considerations to be incorporated into the design and development of technological systems and services from the outset. By prioritizing privacy and data protection during the design phase, organizations can mitigate potential risks and promote responsible data practices. Privacy-enhancing technologies, secure data storage, and robust access controls are examples of measures that can be implemented to ensure privacy by design.

Ethical considerations also extend to the sharing and disclosure of personal data. Organizations should be mindful of the purposes for which data is shared and ensure that data is shared in a secure and responsible manner. An ethical approach involves implementing data sharing agreements, anonymizing or de-identifying data when possible, and adhering to relevant legal and regulatory frameworks to protect individuals' privacy.

Furthermore, the ethical use of surveillance technologies requires careful consideration. Balancing the need for security and public safety with individuals' privacy rights and civil liberties is a complex ethical challenge. Surveillance practices should be guided by clear legal frameworks, oversight mechanisms, and proportionality. Transparency, accountability, and safeguards against abuse are essential to ensure that surveillance is used responsibly and ethically.

In conclusion, ethical considerations in data collection and surveillance are crucial in the digital age. Informed consent, data minimization, accuracy, privacy by design, responsible data sharing, and ethical surveillance practices are all vital aspects that organizations and policymakers should address. By upholding these ethical principles, we can protect individuals' privacy, foster trust, and ensure that data collection and surveillance practices align with our shared values of autonomy, fairness, and respect for fundamental rights.

C. Balancing individual privacy rights and societal needs

Balancing individual privacy rights with societal needs is a complex and challenging task in the digital age. On one hand, protecting individuals' privacy rights is essential for upholding autonomy, dignity, and personal freedom. On the other hand, there are legitimate societal needs, such as public safety, security, and the advancement of scientific research, that may require the collection and use of personal data. Striking the right balance between these competing interests requires thoughtful consideration and a nuanced approach.

Respecting individual privacy rights is of utmost importance. Privacy is a fundamental human right that empowers individuals to control their personal information and maintain a sense of autonomy. It allows individuals to safeguard their identities, protect sensitive data, and make choices about how their personal information is used and shared. Respecting privacy rights helps build trust between individuals and organizations, promoting a healthy and respectful relationship.

At the same time, societal needs cannot be ignored. There are situations where the collection and use of personal data may be necessary to ensure public safety, detect and prevent crimes, or respond effectively to emergencies. For instance, in the context of public health, the collection and analysis of personal data may be crucial for disease surveillance and the development of effective strategies to combat pandemics. In such cases, balancing privacy rights with the greater societal good is a complex ethical challenge.

To strike a balance between individual privacy rights and societal needs, several principles can guide decision-making. One such principle is proportionality, which involves ensuring that the collection and use of personal data are necessary and proportionate to the specific purpose at hand. This requires a careful assessment of the potential benefits and risks associated with data collection and the implementation of measures to minimize privacy infringements.

Another principle is transparency, which entails being open and clear about the purposes and extent of data collection. Organizations and authorities should provide individuals with clear information about why and how their data will be used, enabling them to make informed decisions. Transparency builds trust and allows individuals to understand the trade-offs between privacy rights and societal needs.

Accountability is also essential in balancing privacy rights and societal needs. Organizations and authorities should be accountable for their data practices, ensuring that they comply with applicable laws, regulations, and ethical standards. Accountability involves implementing safeguards, conducting regular privacy assessments, and having mechanisms in place to handle data breaches or misuse.

Moreover, involving individuals in decision-making processes and respecting their preferences can help strike a balance. Individuals should have the opportunity to provide their informed consent or exercise control over the use of their personal data whenever possible. Giving individuals a voice and empowering them to make choices about their privacy can contribute to a more balanced approach that respects both individual rights and societal needs.

In conclusion, balancing individual privacy rights with societal needs is a complex ethical challenge in the digital age. It requires proportionality, transparency, accountability, and respect for individual preferences. By adopting a thoughtful and ethical approach, we can strive to protect privacy rights while addressing legitimate societal needs, fostering a harmonious relationship between privacy and societal interests.

CHAPTER V
AI and Automation Ethics

A. Ethical implications of artificial intelligence

Artificial Intelligence (AI) has rapidly advanced in recent years, bringing with it a host of ethical implications that demand our attention and careful consideration. As AI systems become increasingly capable of mimicking human intelligence and making autonomous decisions, it is essential to examine the ethical dimensions and potential consequences of these technologies.

One of the significant ethical implications of AI is bias and discrimination. AI systems are trained using vast amounts of data, and if that data contains biases or reflects societal inequalities, the AI algorithms may perpetuate and amplify these biases. This can lead to unfair outcomes in areas such as hiring, lending, and criminal justice. Addressing bias in AI requires transparency, fairness, and diversity in data collection, as well as ongoing evaluation and monitoring of AI systems to ensure they do not exacerbate existing societal inequalities.

Another ethical concern is the impact of AI on employment and human autonomy. The increasing automation of tasks raises concerns about job displacement and the potential loss of livelihoods. AI systems that take over decision-making processes may also challenge human autonomy and agency. Ensuring a just transition in the face of automation and protecting human rights and dignity in the workplace are ethical imperatives in the development and deployment of AI technologies.

Transparency and explainability are critical ethical considerations in AI. As AI systems become more complex, it becomes challenging to understand how they reach their decisions or predictions. This lack of transparency can lead to a loss of trust and accountability. Ethical AI systems should be designed to provide explanations for their decisions, allowing individuals to understand and challenge outcomes when necessary.

The ethical implications of AI also extend to privacy and data protection. AI systems often rely on large datasets, which may contain personal and sensitive information. Ensuring that AI systems respect privacy rights, follow data protection regulations, and implement strong security measures is crucial in safeguarding individuals' privacy and maintaining public trust.

Moreover, AI has the potential to disrupt existing power structures and raise questions about accountability. As AI systems take on more decision-making responsibilities, it becomes essential to determine who is accountable for their actions and the potential harm they may cause. Ethical frameworks need to address issues of responsibility, liability, and the development of appropriate legal and regulatory mechanisms to hold individuals, organizations, and algorithms accountable.

Finally, the broader societal impact of AI requires ethical considerations. The deployment of AI can shape social structures, influence public opinion, and impact economic inequality. Ethical AI practices should strive to enhance societal well-being, promote inclusivity, and prioritize the common good. Balancing technological advancements with societal values and the needs of all stakeholders is essential in ensuring that AI benefits society as a whole.

In conclusion, the ethical implications of AI are multifaceted and require careful analysis and ethical frameworks. Addressing issues of bias, job displacement, transparency, privacy, accountability, and the broader societal impact of AI is crucial. By embracing responsible AI practices, we can harness the potential of AI while upholding human values, promoting fairness, and addressing the complex ethical challenges posed by these transformative technologies.

B. Accountability and transparency in AI decision-making

Accountability and transparency are crucial ethical considerations in AI decision-making. As artificial intelligence systems become more advanced and autonomous, it is essential to ensure that they are accountable for their actions and that the decision-making processes are transparent and understandable to stakeholders.

One of the key aspects of accountability in AI is determining who is responsible for the outcomes of AI systems. Traditional models of accountability may not easily apply to AI, as the decision-making process involves complex algorithms and may not be directly attributable to a single individual. Establishing clear lines of accountability requires a collective effort involving developers, organizations, policymakers, and regulatory bodies. It is necessary to define roles and responsibilities, establish mechanisms for oversight, and allocate accountability for the actions and decisions of AI systems.

Transparency is also paramount in ensuring ethical AI decision-making. Transparency refers to the ability to understand and explain how AI systems arrive at their decisions or predictions. Lack of transparency can lead to distrust, as stakeholders may question the fairness and biases embedded within AI algorithms. Ethical AI systems should be designed with transparency in mind, providing explanations and justifications for their decisions in a manner that is understandable to stakeholders. This promotes trust, allows for effective auditing, and enables individuals to challenge outcomes when necessary.

One approach to achieving transparency in AI decision-making is through explainable AI (XAI). XAI aims to develop AI systems that not only provide accurate results but also provide explanations for how those results were derived. By incorporating techniques such as rule-based systems, visualizations, or natural language explanations, AI systems can provide insights into their decision-making processes, increasing transparency and facilitating human understanding.

Furthermore, transparency in AI can be achieved through open data and open source practices. Making data and algorithms publicly available promotes accountability and allows for external scrutiny and evaluation. Openness also encourages collaboration, innovation, and the sharing of best practices among developers and researchers, fostering a more ethical and responsible AI ecosystem.

Accountability and transparency in AI decision-making are crucial for addressing ethical concerns such as bias, discrimination, and the potential harm caused by AI systems. By ensuring that AI systems can be held accountable and their decision-making processes are transparent, we can mitigate risks, promote fairness, and build trust between AI systems and the individuals and communities they affect. Striving for accountability and transparency is essential in harnessing the power of AI while upholding ethical principles and protecting the rights and well-being of individuals in the digital age.

C. Social and economic impact of automation

The social and economic impact of automation is a significant ethical consideration in the age of AI and automation. As technology advances and automation becomes more prevalent, it has the potential to reshape industries, employment, and society at large. Examining the social and economic implications is crucial to ensure that the benefits of automation are distributed equitably and that the potential negative consequences are mitigated.

One of the primary social impacts of automation is the potential displacement of jobs. As tasks that were previously performed by humans are automated, there is a risk of job loss in certain sectors. This raises concerns about unemployment, income inequality, and the need for retraining and reskilling programs. Ethical considerations involve ensuring a just transition for workers, promoting lifelong learning, and creating new opportunities in emerging industries.

Automation also has the potential to exacerbate existing social inequalities. Certain demographics and communities may be disproportionately affected by job displacement or may lack access to the benefits and opportunities that automation brings. Ethical considerations involve addressing these disparities, promoting inclusivity, and ensuring that the benefits of automation are shared equitably across society. This may involve targeted policies, investment in education and infrastructure, and efforts to bridge the digital divide.

Furthermore, the economic impact of automation can lead to a concentration of wealth and power. Industries that successfully adopt automation technologies may experience increased productivity and profitability, leading to wealth accumulation for the owners and shareholders. Ethical considerations involve assessing the distribution of economic benefits and ensuring that the gains from automation are not concentrated in the hands of a few. This may involve mechanisms such as fair taxation, income redistribution, and the exploration of alternative economic models that prioritize societal well-being.

Automation also has the potential to change the nature of work and the skills required in the labor market. As routine and repetitive tasks become automated, there is an increasing demand for skills that complement and collaborate with AI technologies. Ethical considerations involve promoting education and training programs that equip individuals with the skills needed in an automated workforce. Additionally, fostering a culture of lifelong learning and adaptability is crucial to ensure that individuals can thrive in an evolving job market.

Moreover, automation can impact the overall quality of work and job satisfaction. While automation can eliminate mundane and repetitive tasks, it may also lead to a loss of autonomy, creativity, and job security for some workers. Ethical considerations involve designing automation technologies and workplace policies that prioritize human well-being, job satisfaction, and meaningful work. Ensuring that workers have a voice in shaping automation processes and that human-centric values are upheld is essential in maintaining a healthy and ethical work environment.

In conclusion, the social and economic impact of automation raises ethical considerations that require careful attention. Balancing the benefits of automation with concerns such as job displacement, inequality, economic concentration, skills development, and job quality is essential.

CHAPTER VI
Bias and Discrimination in Technology

A. Understanding bias in algorithms and machine learning

Bias in algorithms and machine learning is a critical ethical issue that needs to be addressed in the development and deployment of technology. Algorithms, which form the basis of many automated decision-making systems, can inadvertently reflect and perpetuate biases present in the data they are trained on or the design choices made during their development.

Understanding bias in algorithms and machine learning begins with recognizing that bias can manifest in multiple forms. One common type of bias is data bias, which occurs when the training data used to build the algorithm is unrepresentative or contains systemic biases. If the training data is skewed towards certain demographics or lacks diversity, the algorithm may produce biased outcomes, reinforcing existing inequalities.

Algorithmic bias can also result from biased design decisions or the way in which the algorithm is trained and evaluated. For example, if a facial recognition algorithm is primarily trained on data from one racial or ethnic group, it may exhibit higher error rates and misidentification for other groups. Similarly, biases can be introduced through the selection of certain features or variables in the algorithm, leading to discriminatory outcomes.

The consequences of algorithmic bias can be far-reaching. Biased algorithms can perpetuate and amplify existing social inequalities, affecting areas such as hiring, lending, criminal justice, and access to services. For instance, biased algorithms used in hiring processes may disadvantage certain demographic groups, resulting in discriminatory hiring practices. Such biases can further entrench societal disparities and hinder progress towards a fair and equitable society.

Addressing bias in algorithms and machine learning requires a multi-faceted approach. It starts with acknowledging the presence of bias and actively working towards reducing its impact. This includes collecting diverse and representative training data, regularly auditing algorithms for biases, and conducting thorough evaluations to assess the fairness and equity of algorithmic outcomes.

Increasing transparency and explainability in algorithms is also crucial. By providing insights into the decision-making process, individuals and organizations can better understand the potential biases at play and challenge unjust outcomes. This transparency enables accountability and fosters trust between users and the technology they interact with.

Additionally, promoting diversity and inclusivity in the development and evaluation of algorithms is vital. Bringing diverse perspectives and expertise to the table helps identify and mitigate biases that might be overlooked otherwise. It is important to involve individuals from different backgrounds and communities to ensure that biases are recognized and addressed from the early stages of algorithm development.

Ongoing research, collaboration, and sharing of best practices in the field of algorithmic fairness are essential in combating bias. Researchers, policymakers, and industry professionals must collaborate to develop robust methods for detecting and mitigating bias in algorithms. By continuously improving and refining our understanding of bias, we can work towards creating more fair and unbiased technological systems.

In conclusion, understanding bias in algorithms and machine learning is critical in addressing the ethical challenges it poses. By recognizing the various forms of bias, promoting transparency and inclusivity, and actively working towards reducing bias in algorithms, we can develop and deploy technology that respects and upholds the principles of fairness, equity, and non-discrimination.

B. Ethical challenges related to discrimination in technology

Ethical challenges related to discrimination in technology are of great concern as technology increasingly influences various aspects of our lives. Discrimination can occur when technological systems or algorithms perpetuate biases or treat individuals unfairly based on protected characteristics such as race, gender, age, or religion. These challenges demand careful examination to ensure fairness, equal treatment, and respect for individual rights.

One ethical challenge is the unintentional amplification of existing societal biases through technological systems. If the data used to train algorithms reflects historical biases and discriminatory practices, the algorithms can inadvertently perpetuate those biases. For example, if a hiring algorithm is trained on data that favors certain demographics due to historical patterns, it can lead to biased hiring decisions and perpetuate discriminatory practices in the workplace.

Another challenge is the lack of diversity and inclusion in the development and testing of technology. When technology is designed and implemented without diverse perspectives, it can inadvertently overlook the needs and experiences of marginalized communities. This can result in exclusionary or discriminatory outcomes. Ethical considerations call for promoting diversity in technology development teams, involving users from diverse backgrounds, and conducting thorough evaluations to identify and address discriminatory impacts.

The potential for disparate impact is another ethical challenge. Disparate impact occurs when a seemingly neutral technological system has a disproportionately negative impact on certain groups, even if discrimination is not intended. For example, an automated loan approval system may have a higher rejection rate for applicants from certain racial or socioeconomic backgrounds, leading to unequal access to financial resources. Addressing disparate impact requires a proactive approach to ensure that technological systems do not perpetuate systemic inequalities.

Transparency and explainability are key ethical challenges related to discrimination in technology. When decisions are made by algorithms or automated systems, it is important for individuals to understand how those decisions are reached and whether they are fair and unbiased. Lack of transparency can erode trust and hinder individuals' ability to challenge discriminatory outcomes. Ethical considerations involve ensuring that algorithms are explainable, providing individuals with information about the decision-making process, and enabling them to seek redress in cases of discrimination.

Moreover, there is an ethical challenge related to the accountability of technology developers and providers for discriminatory outcomes. As technology becomes more complex and autonomous, it can be difficult to assign responsibility when discrimination occurs. Ethical frameworks need to address issues of accountability, liability, and the development of appropriate legal and regulatory mechanisms to hold individuals, organizations, and algorithms accountable for discriminatory actions.

Mitigating the ethical challenges related to discrimination in technology requires a combination of technical, social, and legal measures. It involves proactive efforts to reduce biases in data, promote diversity in technology development, ensure transparency and explainability in algorithmic decision-making, and establish mechanisms for accountability and redress. By addressing these challenges, we can strive for technology that respects the dignity, equality, and rights of all individuals and contributes to a more inclusive and just society.

C. Promoting fairness and inclusivity in technological systems

Promoting fairness and inclusivity in technological systems is a crucial ethical imperative in addressing the challenges of bias and discrimination. As technology plays an increasingly influential role in society, it is essential to design, develop, and deploy technological systems in a manner that respects diversity, upholds equality, and ensures equitable outcomes for all individuals.

One approach to promoting fairness and inclusivity is through data collection and representation. It is important to collect diverse and representative data to mitigate biases and ensure that technological systems capture the experiences, perspectives, and needs of all individuals. This involves actively seeking out and including data from underrepresented groups to avoid perpetuating existing inequalities. Ethical considerations call for the responsible collection and use of data, paying attention to data quality, inclusivity, and the potential impact on marginalized communities.

The development and testing of technological systems should involve diverse teams that reflect the broader population. By incorporating a variety of perspectives, experiences, and expertise, biases and blind spots can be identified and addressed more effectively. Diverse teams are more likely to recognize and challenge discriminatory outcomes, leading to the creation of fairer and more inclusive technological systems.

Transparency is another crucial aspect of promoting fairness and inclusivity. Making the decision-making processes of technological systems transparent allows individuals to understand how outcomes are determined and whether they are fair. Providing explanations and justifications for decisions allows for accountability and empowers individuals to challenge discriminatory practices. Transparency builds trust and fosters a sense of agency among users, ensuring that technological systems are accountable to the people they impact.

Additionally, ongoing evaluation and monitoring of technological systems are essential to identify and rectify biases or discriminatory outcomes. Regular assessments can help uncover unintended consequences, disparate impacts, or biases that emerge over time. Ethical considerations call for continuous monitoring to ensure that the outcomes produced by technological systems remain fair and equitable, and to allow for corrective actions when biases are detected.

Human oversight and intervention are crucial in promoting fairness and inclusivity. While automation and AI can bring efficiencies and advancements, it is important to maintain human judgment and decision-making in critical areas to prevent the entrenchment of biases. Human intervention provides a means to review, challenge, and correct algorithmic decisions, ensuring that human values and ethical considerations are upheld.

Moreover, engaging with affected communities and seeking their input is essential in promoting fairness and inclusivity. By involving users and stakeholders from diverse backgrounds, technology developers can gain valuable insights, understand specific needs and concerns, and co-create solutions that cater to a broad range of individuals. Engaging in meaningful dialogue and incorporating user feedback enables the development of technological systems that are truly inclusive and responsive to diverse needs.

In conclusion, promoting fairness and inclusivity in technological systems requires a holistic approach that encompasses data collection, diverse development teams, transparency, evaluation, human oversight, and community engagement. By addressing biases, rectifying discriminatory outcomes, and involving stakeholders in the design and development process, we can create technological systems that advance fairness, equality, and inclusivity. Ethical considerations must guide the development and use of technology to ensure that it respects the rights, dignity, and well-being of all individuals in our diverse and interconnected world.

CHAPTER VIII
Internet and Digital Media Ethics

A. Freedom of speech and censorship on the internet

Freedom of speech and censorship on the internet are vital ethical considerations in the realm of internet and digital media ethics. The internet has revolutionized the way information is disseminated and consumed, offering a platform for individuals to express their views and engage in open discourse. However, this freedom also raises questions about the boundaries of expression, the impact of harmful content, and the role of platforms in regulating speech.

Freedom of speech is a fundamental human right that allows individuals to express their opinions, ideas, and beliefs without fear of censorship or retribution. The internet has provided a powerful avenue for free expression, enabling individuals to share information, voice dissent, and engage in public dialogue on a global scale. This freedom fosters creativity, innovation, and the exchange of diverse perspectives, contributing to the growth of knowledge and democratic participation.

However, freedom of speech on the internet is not without its challenges. The ease and speed with which information can spread online have led to the dissemination of harmful content, including hate speech, misinformation, and online harassment. Balancing the principles of free expression with the need to protect individuals from harm and maintain a healthy online environment is an ongoing ethical dilemma.

Censorship on the internet refers to the regulation and control of information flow, often by governments, organizations, or online platforms. While some argue that certain limitations on speech are necessary to protect public safety, privacy, and individual rights, others emphasize the importance of maintaining an open and inclusive digital space that allows for robust debate and the free exchange of ideas.

The ethical challenges of freedom of speech and censorship on the internet involve finding the right balance between protecting individuals from harm and upholding the principles of free expression. It requires careful consideration of the context, intent, and potential impact of speech, as well as the responsibilities of online platforms in moderating content.

Online platforms play a significant role in shaping the digital media landscape and have a responsibility to implement policies and guidelines that promote a safe and inclusive environment while respecting freedom of speech. Ethical considerations call for transparent and consistent moderation practices that address harmful content without unduly restricting legitimate expression. It is important for platforms to strike a balance between protecting users from hate speech, harassment, and harmful misinformation while avoiding arbitrary or biased censorship.

Moreover, the regulation of speech on the Internet should be guided by democratic principles, the rule of law, and respect for human rights. Governments and regulatory bodies have a responsibility to develop clear legal frameworks that define the boundaries of permissible speech while safeguarding freedom of expression. These frameworks should be transparent, subject to public debate, and designed to protect individuals' rights and promote a diverse and pluralistic digital environment.

Education and digital literacy also play a crucial role in addressing the ethical challenges of freedom of speech and censorship. Empowering individuals to critically evaluate and navigate online content, recognize misinformation, and engage in respectful and constructive dialogue can help mitigate the negative impacts of harmful speech while preserving the principles of free expression.

In conclusion, freedom of speech and censorship on the internet are complex ethical considerations. Upholding the principles of free expression while addressing the challenges of harmful content and maintaining a safe online environment require thoughtful approaches. Striking a balance between protecting individuals from harm and ensuring an open and inclusive digital space requires transparent moderation practices, democratic legal frameworks, and a commitment to digital literacy. Ethical considerations must guide the development and implementation of policies and practices that respect freedom of speech while upholding the well-being and rights of individuals in the digital age.

B. Fake news and disinformation in the digital age

Fake news and disinformation in the digital age pose significant ethical challenges in the realm of internet and digital media ethics. The rapid spread and consumption of misinformation have the potential to undermine public trust, distort reality, and manipulate public opinion. Addressing the ethical implications of fake news and disinformation requires a multi-faceted approach that involves media literacy, responsible information sharing, and the responsibility of platforms and individuals in combating this issue.

Fake news refers to false or misleading information presented as legitimate news. It can be created and spread with malicious intent or simply due to a lack of journalistic rigor and verification. The digital age has made it easier for fake news to circulate, as information can be disseminated rapidly through social media and other online platforms. The ethical challenge lies in the potential harm caused by fake news, including the erosion of trust, the spread of misinformation on critical issues, and the manipulation of public opinion.

Disinformation, on the other hand, refers to the deliberate spread of false or misleading information with the intention to deceive or manipulate. It is often used as a tool to achieve specific political, social, or economic objectives. The ethical concerns surrounding disinformation are rooted in its ability to undermine democratic processes, stoke division, and influence public perception and decision-making.

To address the ethical challenges of fake news and disinformation, media literacy plays a crucial role. Promoting media literacy empowers individuals to critically evaluate information, discern credible sources, and understand the techniques used to manipulate or deceive. Education and awareness campaigns can equip individuals with the skills to navigate the digital media landscape responsibly, empowering them to identify and combat fake news and disinformation.

Responsible information sharing is another ethical consideration. Individuals have a responsibility to verify the accuracy of the information they share and to consider the potential consequences of spreading false or misleading content. Engaging in fact-checking, cross-referencing sources, and promoting accuracy and credibility in information sharing can contribute to combating the spread of fake news and disinformation.

Platforms and technology companies also bear a significant responsibility in addressing fake news and disinformation. They play a central role in the distribution and visibility of content, and therefore have the power to influence the spread of misinformation. Ethical considerations call for platforms to implement robust content moderation policies, fact-checking mechanisms, and transparency in algorithmic decisions. Collaboration between platforms, fact-checking organizations, and other stakeholders can help identify and mitigate the impact of fake news and disinformation.

Additionally, promoting a culture of responsible journalism and media ethics is crucial. Media organizations have a responsibility to uphold journalistic integrity, adhere to ethical guidelines, and prioritize accuracy and truthfulness in their reporting. Journalistic standards and practices, including fact-checking, verification, and responsible sourcing, are essential in combating fake news and disinformation.

In conclusion, fake news and disinformation in the digital age present significant ethical challenges. Addressing these challenges requires a combination of media literacy, responsible information sharing, responsible platform policies, and a commitment to journalistic integrity. By empowering individuals, promoting critical thinking, and fostering responsible media practices, we can work towards a more informed and resilient society that is better equipped to combat the spread of fake news and disinformation in the digital age.

C. Ethical responsibilities of users and platforms

The ethical responsibilities of both users and platforms in the realm of internet and digital media ethics are crucial for promoting a safe, inclusive, and responsible online environment. Users and platforms share a collective responsibility to uphold ethical standards, respect the rights of others, and contribute to the positive impact of digital media.

Users have ethical responsibilities when it comes to their online behavior and the content they generate and share. They should strive to engage in respectful and constructive dialogue, treating others with dignity and empathy. Ethical considerations call for users to verify the accuracy of information before sharing it, to avoid spreading misinformation or contributing to the dissemination of fake news. Users should also be aware of the potential consequences of their online actions, including the impact of their words and the potential harm caused by cyberbullying, harassment, or hate speech. Taking personal responsibility for one's online presence and striving to contribute positively to the digital community are essential ethical obligations for users.

Platforms, as intermediaries and facilitators of online communication, bear significant ethical responsibilities as well. They have a duty to implement robust content moderation policies that prioritize user safety, respect for human rights, and the prevention of harm. This includes combating hate speech, harassment, and the spread of harmful or illegal content. Platforms should also prioritize transparency in their algorithms and recommendation systems to mitigate the risk of filter bubbles and echo chambers, which can contribute to the polarization of opinions and the spread of disinformation. Ethical considerations call for platforms to actively engage with user feedback and address concerns promptly, ensuring that users have avenues for reporting abusive or inappropriate behavior. Additionally, platforms should respect user privacy, handle personal data responsibly, and be transparent about data collection and usage practices.

Collaboration between users and platforms is essential in fostering an ethical digital media landscape. Users can hold platforms accountable by providing feedback, reporting violations of community guidelines, and advocating for responsible platform policies. Platforms, in turn, can work with users to develop features, tools, and policies that address emerging ethical challenges and promote a safe and inclusive online environment.

Furthermore, platforms have a responsibility to promote digital literacy and empower users to navigate the digital landscape responsibly. This can be achieved through educational initiatives, providing clear guidelines and resources on responsible online behavior, and promoting media literacy to enhance users' critical thinking skills and their ability to discern credible sources from misinformation.

In conclusion, the ethical responsibilities of users and platforms in internet and digital media ethics are intertwined. Users must engage in responsible online behavior, promote empathy and respect, and contribute positively to the digital community. Platforms, as intermediaries, have the responsibility to implement ethical content moderation policies, prioritize user safety, and promote transparency and accountability. Through collaboration and a shared commitment to ethical principles, users and platforms can work together to create a digital media environment that upholds human rights, fosters inclusivity, and promotes responsible digital citizenship.

CHAPTER IX
Cybersecurity and Ethical Hacking

A. Importance of cybersecurity in the digital age

Cybersecurity plays a critical role in the digital age, where our lives are increasingly intertwined with technology. The importance of cybersecurity cannot be overstated, as it encompasses the protection of sensitive information, the safeguarding of digital infrastructure, and the preservation of privacy and trust in the digital realm.

One of the primary reasons why cybersecurity is essential is the protection of sensitive data. In today's digital landscape, individuals, businesses, and governments rely on the secure storage and transmission of vast amounts of data. This data may include personal information, financial records, trade secrets, intellectual property, and much more. Without adequate cybersecurity measures in place, this data is susceptible to theft, misuse, or unauthorized access, which can result in financial loss, reputational damage, and privacy violations.

Cybersecurity is also crucial for safeguarding digital infrastructure. Our interconnected world heavily relies on critical infrastructure systems, such as power grids, transportation networks, healthcare systems, and communication networks. These systems are vulnerable to cyberattacks that can disrupt essential services, cause economic damage, or compromise public safety. By investing in robust cybersecurity measures, we can protect these critical infrastructures and ensure their uninterrupted operation.

Preserving privacy is another significant aspect of cybersecurity. In an era where personal information is collected, stored, and shared extensively, maintaining privacy is essential for individual autonomy, dignity, and freedom. Cybersecurity measures, such as encryption, secure communication protocols, and access controls, help safeguard personal data from unauthorized access, surveillance, and breaches of privacy.

Moreover, cybersecurity is instrumental in maintaining trust and confidence in the digital realm. As individuals, businesses, and governments rely on digital transactions, online services, and communication platforms, trust in the security of these systems is paramount. Cybersecurity measures, along with transparent practices and a proactive response to cyber threats, build trust among users and stakeholders, fostering a sense of security and reliability in the digital ecosystem.

Cybersecurity also has societal implications. As cyber threats continue to evolve and cybercriminals become more sophisticated, the protection of individuals, communities, and nations against cyberattacks is a collective responsibility. By prioritizing cybersecurity, governments can ensure the resilience of their nations' digital infrastructure, protect national security, and promote economic stability. Collaboration between governments, businesses, and individuals is crucial in addressing cybersecurity challenges and creating a secure digital environment for all.

In conclusion, the importance of cybersecurity in the digital age cannot be overstated. It encompasses the protection of sensitive data, the safeguarding of digital infrastructure, the preservation of privacy, and the promotion of trust and confidence in the digital realm. By investing in robust cybersecurity measures, promoting awareness, and fostering collaboration, we can mitigate cyber risks and ensure a safe and secure digital landscape for individuals, businesses, and societies as a whole.

B. Ethical hacking and its role in protecting against cyber threats

Ethical hacking, also known as white-hat hacking or penetration testing, plays a crucial role in protecting against cyber threats and enhancing cybersecurity. Ethical hackers are skilled professionals who use their expertise to identify vulnerabilities and weaknesses in computer systems, networks, and software applications. By intentionally and lawfully exploiting these vulnerabilities, ethical hackers help organizations understand their security weaknesses, fix them, and strengthen their defenses against malicious attacks.

The role of ethical hacking is multifaceted. Firstly, ethical hackers act as proactive defenders, taking a preemptive approach to cybersecurity. By simulating real-world attacks, they identify potential entry points and vulnerabilities that malicious hackers could exploit. This allows organizations to patch these vulnerabilities before they are exploited, preventing potential breaches and minimizing the risk of data theft, unauthorized access, or system disruption.

Ethical hackers also contribute to improving overall system security and resilience. By uncovering vulnerabilities and weaknesses, they provide organizations with valuable insights and recommendations for improving their security posture. This includes suggesting security controls, implementing best practices, and raising awareness about potential risks. Ethical hacking helps organizations understand their security gaps and develop robust defense mechanisms to protect against evolving cyber threats.

Another critical role of ethical hacking is ensuring compliance with security standards and regulations. Many industries, such as finance, healthcare, and government, are subject to strict regulatory requirements to protect sensitive information. Ethical hacking helps organizations meet these compliance obligations by identifying areas of non-compliance and recommending appropriate measures to address them.

Ethical hackers also contribute to creating a security-conscious culture within organizations. Their findings and recommendations serve as educational tools, raising awareness among employees about the importance of cybersecurity and the potential risks they may encounter. This awareness helps foster a proactive mindset towards security, encouraging individuals to be vigilant, practice secure behavior, and report potential vulnerabilities or suspicious activities.

Furthermore, ethical hacking plays a vital role in the ongoing improvement of cybersecurity practices. As new threats and attack techniques emerge, ethical hackers stay up-to-date with the latest trends and vulnerabilities. They continually adapt their skills and techniques to identify new attack vectors, ensuring that organizations remain prepared and resilient in the face of evolving cyber threats.

It is worth noting that ethical hacking operates within a legal and ethical framework. Ethical hackers obtain proper authorization from organizations before conducting security assessments, ensuring that their actions comply with applicable laws and regulations. Their goal is not to cause harm or exploit vulnerabilities for personal gain, but rather to improve security, protect data, and promote a safer digital environment.

In conclusion, ethical hacking plays a critical role in protecting against cyber threats. By identifying vulnerabilities, recommending security measures, raising awareness, and enhancing system resilience, ethical hackers help organizations stay one step ahead of malicious attackers. Their proactive approach and commitment to ethical standards contribute to the overall improvement of cybersecurity practices, fostering a safer and more secure digital landscape for individuals, businesses, and societies.

C. Balancing security and privacy concerns

Balancing security and privacy concerns is a complex ethical challenge in the realm of cybersecurity and ethical hacking. While ensuring robust security measures is crucial for protecting sensitive data and preventing cyber threats, it is equally important to respect individuals' privacy rights and maintain the confidentiality of their personal information. Striking the right balance between security and privacy requires careful consideration of ethical principles, legal frameworks, and technological solutions.

Security measures are implemented to safeguard against cyber threats, such as unauthorized access, data breaches, and malicious attacks. Organizations and individuals have a responsibility to protect their systems, networks, and data from these threats. This may involve employing encryption, access controls, firewalls, intrusion detection systems, and other security technologies. These measures help mitigate risks and safeguard sensitive information.

However, security measures must be implemented in a manner that respects privacy rights and minimizes unnecessary intrusion. It is important to avoid overreach and the indiscriminate collection or monitoring of personal data, as this can infringe upon privacy rights and erode trust. Ethical considerations call for organizations and individuals to collect and process only the necessary data required for legitimate security purposes, and to handle that data responsibly and transparently.

Furthermore, privacy-enhancing technologies can play a crucial role in striking the balance between security and privacy. Technologies such as differential privacy, data anonymization, and secure multiparty computation allow for the protection of privacy while still enabling effective security measures. These technologies aim to minimize the disclosure of personally identifiable information and ensure that security measures are implemented in a privacy-preserving manner.

Legal and regulatory frameworks also provide guidance in balancing security and privacy concerns. Laws and regulations, such as the General Data Protection Regulation (GDPR) and the California Consumer Privacy Act (CCPA), outline privacy rights, data protection principles, and requirements for handling personal information. Organizations and individuals must comply with these regulations and incorporate privacy considerations into their security practices.

Transparency and informed consent are fundamental ethical principles in balancing security and privacy. Individuals should be informed about the collection, use, and storage of their personal data and have the ability to provide informed consent for data processing. Organizations should communicate their security practices and privacy policies clearly, ensuring individuals have the necessary information to make informed decisions regarding their privacy.

Open dialogue and collaboration between security professionals, privacy advocates, policymakers, and technology developers are essential in addressing the ethical challenges of balancing security and privacy. Engaging in conversations about best practices, ethical frameworks, and legal requirements helps identify areas of potential conflict and explore solutions that prioritize both security and privacy.

In conclusion, balancing security and privacy concerns requires a thoughtful and ethical approach. Organizations and individuals must implement security measures to protect against cyber threats while respecting privacy rights and minimizing unnecessary intrusion. Privacy-enhancing technologies, legal frameworks, transparency, and informed consent all contribute to finding the right equilibrium between security and privacy. By upholding these principles and engaging in collaborative discussions, we can create a digital landscape that ensures both security and privacy, promoting trust, confidentiality, and the protection of individual rights.

CHAPTER X
Future Ethical Challenges

A. Emerging technologies and their ethical implications

Emerging technologies present a host of new ethical challenges that require careful consideration and proactive measures. As society continues to embrace advancements in fields such as artificial intelligence, blockchain, virtual reality, genetic engineering, and autonomous systems, it is crucial to anticipate and address the ethical implications that arise alongside these technologies.

Artificial intelligence (AI), for example, raises concerns regarding the potential for bias, discrimination, and loss of human control. As AI systems make decisions that impact individuals' lives, ethical considerations call for transparency, accountability, and fairness in algorithmic decision-making. Additionally, the ethical dilemmas surrounding AI include the potential for job displacement, the responsible development of autonomous vehicles, and the ethical boundaries of AI in areas such as healthcare and warfare.

Blockchain technology, while offering opportunities for decentralized and secure transactions, raises ethical questions related to privacy, data protection, and the use of cryptocurrencies in illicit activities. Balancing the potential benefits of blockchain with the need to protect individuals' rights and prevent misuse is a critical ethical challenge.

Virtual reality (VR) and augmented reality (AR) technologies present ethical considerations in areas such as privacy, consent, and the blurring of the line between virtual and real-world experiences. The immersive nature of these technologies raises questions about informed consent, the protection of personal data, and the potential psychological impacts on individuals.

Genetic engineering and biotechnology advancements introduce ethical dilemmas regarding the ethical boundaries of manipulating DNA, such as gene editing, human cloning, and genetic enhancement. Questions arise about the potential for creating designer babies, the fairness of access to genetic therapies, and the long-term consequences of genetic modifications.

Autonomous systems, including autonomous vehicles and drones, bring ethical challenges related to safety, accountability, and decision-making. The ethical implications of accidents involving autonomous vehicles, the use of autonomous drones in warfare, and the potential for biased or unethical decision-making algorithms in autonomous systems are areas that require careful consideration.

Additionally, the convergence of technologies and the creation of new interdisciplinary fields, such as the Internet of Things (IoT), biometrics, and brain-computer interfaces, present ethical challenges related to privacy, consent, security, and the potential for misuse of personal data.

Addressing these emerging ethical challenges requires a multidisciplinary and collaborative approach. It involves engaging diverse stakeholders, including scientists, technologists, policymakers, ethicists, and the public, in dialogue and decision-making processes. Ethical frameworks, guidelines, and regulations should be developed to ensure the responsible and ethical development, deployment, and use of emerging technologies.

Education and awareness play a crucial role in navigating future ethical challenges. By promoting digital literacy, critical thinking, and ethical reasoning, individuals can better understand the implications of emerging technologies and make informed decisions regarding their adoption and use. Ethical considerations must be integrated into the education and training of professionals working in fields impacted by emerging technologies.

In conclusion, emerging technologies bring forth a range of ethical challenges that require proactive and thoughtful approaches. Anticipating and addressing the ethical implications of AI, blockchain, VR, genetic engineering, autonomous systems, and other emerging fields is essential for ensuring that these technologies are developed and utilized in ways that promote human well-being, respect individual rights, and uphold ethical principles. By engaging in ongoing dialogue, collaboration, and education, we can navigate these challenges and shape a future where emerging technologies are harnessed for the greater good.

B. Anticipating and addressing future moral dilemmas

Anticipating and addressing future moral dilemmas is crucial as society navigates the ever-evolving landscape of technology and its impact on various aspects of our lives. By proactively identifying potential ethical challenges, we can develop strategies and frameworks to address them effectively and ensure that technological advancements align with our shared values and principles.

One future moral dilemma is the ethical implications of advanced AI systems. As AI continues to progress, questions arise regarding the ethical boundaries of AI capabilities, the potential for AI to surpass human intelligence, and the implications for human autonomy and decision-making. Anticipating and addressing these dilemmas involves establishing guidelines and principles that govern the development and deployment of AI technologies, ensuring transparency, fairness, and accountability.

Another moral dilemma relates to the ethical use of personal data and privacy in an increasingly connected world. As technology becomes more integrated into our daily lives, the collection and utilization of personal data raise concerns about surveillance, data breaches, and the erosion of privacy rights. Addressing these dilemmas requires robust privacy regulations, responsible data management practices, and empowering individuals with control over their personal information.

The ethical challenges associated with genetic engineering and biotechnology also demand attention. As genetic technologies advance, questions arise regarding the ethical boundaries of modifying human genes, the potential for genetic discrimination, and the implications for future generations. Anticipating and addressing these dilemmas involves engaging in public discourse, establishing regulatory frameworks, and ensuring that ethical considerations guide the responsible use of genetic technologies.

In the realm of digital media and social platforms, the ethical challenges of misinformation, online harassment, and algorithmic biases are expected to persist and evolve. As fake news and disinformation continue to spread, it becomes crucial to develop strategies to promote media literacy, critical thinking, and responsible information sharing. Additionally, addressing the ethical dilemmas surrounding online harassment and algorithmic biases requires comprehensive policies, user empowerment, and platform accountability.

Furthermore, the ethical implications of emerging technologies such as virtual reality, augmented reality, and brain-computer interfaces need careful consideration. These technologies raise questions about informed consent, the blurring of virtual and real-world experiences, and the potential impacts on individual well-being and agency. Anticipating and addressing these dilemmas involves interdisciplinary collaboration, public engagement, and the development of ethical guidelines and safeguards.

In addressing future moral dilemmas, it is essential to prioritize inclusivity and avoid exacerbating existing societal inequalities. Technology should be developed and deployed in a manner that is accessible to all, considers diverse perspectives, and actively addresses biases and discrimination.

Ultimately, anticipating and addressing future moral dilemmas requires an ongoing commitment to ethical reflection, stakeholder engagement, and the integration of ethical considerations into the design, development, and deployment of new technologies. By proactively engaging with these challenges, we can shape a future that is guided by our shared values, respects individual rights, and ensures the well-being and flourishing of all individuals and society as a whole.

C. Ethical considerations for the future of technology

Ethical considerations for the future of technology are essential in ensuring that technological advancements align with our values, promote human well-being, and avoid potential harm. As we navigate the path of technological progress, several key ethical considerations emerge.

Firstly, inclusivity and equitable access to technology are crucial ethical considerations. As technology continues to shape various aspects of our lives, it is essential to bridge the digital divide and ensure that advancements are accessible to all individuals, regardless of socioeconomic status, geography, or other factors. Efforts should be made to minimize disparities and ensure that technology does not exacerbate existing inequalities.

Responsible innovation is another important ethical consideration. The rapid pace of technological advancements can outpace our ability to fully understand their implications. Ethical considerations call for responsible research and development practices, including thorough risk assessments, transparency, and ongoing monitoring of the societal impact of new technologies. Collaboration between technologists, policymakers, and ethicists is vital in establishing ethical guidelines and frameworks for responsible innovation.

Safeguarding privacy and data protection remains a critical ethical concern. As technology collects and processes vast amounts of personal data, individuals must have control over their information and understand how it is used. Ethical considerations call for robust privacy policies, informed consent mechanisms, and secure data storage and handling practices. Organizations and policymakers must prioritize data protection to maintain individuals' trust and confidence in the digital landscape.

Transparency and accountability in algorithmic decision-making are also important ethical considerations. As algorithms increasingly shape our lives, there is a need for transparency in how decisions are made, especially when they impact individuals' rights and opportunities. Ethical considerations call for explanations of algorithmic processes, auditing mechanisms, and the ability to contest or challenge automated decisions. Fairness, accountability, and avoiding algorithmic biases are essential in ensuring that technology serves the best interests of all individuals.

The ethical challenges of technology's impact on employment and the workforce require careful attention. As automation and artificial intelligence continue to advance, there are concerns about job displacement and the ethical implications for workers. Ethical considerations call for measures such as reskilling programs, social safety nets, and the thoughtful integration of technology to ensure a just and equitable transition for workers.

Additionally, the ethical considerations of technology's environmental impact are increasingly prominent. As technology evolves, there is a need to minimize its carbon footprint, address electronic waste, and develop sustainable practices. Ethical considerations call for environmentally responsible design, responsible manufacturing processes, and the promotion of circular economy principles in the technology sector.

Ultimately, addressing the ethical considerations for the future of technology requires a multidimensional approach that incorporates diverse perspectives, engages stakeholders, and promotes public dialogue.

Ethical principles and guidelines should guide the development, deployment, and use of technology to ensure that it serves the greater good, respects individual rights, and advances human well-being. By fostering an ethical foundation for the future of technology, we can shape a future that is both technologically advanced and ethically sound.

Conclusion

Recap of key ethical dilemmas discussed

Throughout this exploration of tech ethics in the digital age, we have delved into key ethical dilemmas that arise from the rapid advancements in technology. Let us recap these significant ethical challenges that demand our attention and thoughtful consideration.

We began by recognizing the importance of technology ethics in the digital age, emphasizing the need to navigate the moral dilemmas that emerge alongside technological progress. In our discussion, we explored the definition of technology ethics, acknowledging that it involves the study of ethical principles and frameworks that guide our behavior and decision-making in the realm of technology.

We then moved on to discuss the moral dilemmas faced in the digital age, highlighting the complex issues surrounding privacy and data ethics. The importance of privacy in the digital age became apparent, along with the ethical considerations in data collection, surveillance, and striking a balance between individual privacy rights and societal needs.

The impact of technology on society was another critical aspect we explored, uncovering both the positive and negative effects of technology. We examined how technology has transformed various domains, from communication and productivity to healthcare and entertainment. It was essential to acknowledge the ethical implications of technological advancements, particularly in relation to social and economic aspects.

Ethical frameworks for the digital age provided us with valuable tools for navigating technology ethics. We explored utilitarianism, deontological ethics, and virtue ethics, recognizing the relevance and applicability of these frameworks in making ethical decisions related to technology.

Our exploration then led us to discuss AI and automation ethics, shedding light on the ethical implications of artificial intelligence, accountability and transparency in

AI decision-making, and the social and economic impact of automation.

Bias and discrimination in technology emerged as another pressing concern, as we delved into the understanding of bias in algorithms and machine learning, the ethical challenges associated with discrimination in technology, and the promotion of fairness and inclusivity in technological systems.

We then turned our attention to internet and digital media ethics, recognizing the significance of freedom of speech and censorship on the internet, the challenges posed by fake news and disinformation, and the ethical responsibilities of users and platforms in maintaining a safe and inclusive online environment.

Cybersecurity and ethical hacking were highlighted as critical areas in safeguarding against cyber threats. We discussed the importance of cybersecurity in the digital age, the role of ethical hacking in protecting against cyber threats, and the ethical considerations in balancing security and privacy concerns.

Lastly, we contemplated the future ethical challenges that await us, addressing emerging technologies and their ethical implications, anticipating and addressing future moral dilemmas, and discussing the ethical considerations for the future of technology.

Through our exploration, it became evident that tech ethics is a dynamic and evolving field, demanding continuous reflection, dialogue, and ethical decision-making. By understanding and addressing these ethical dilemmas, we can shape a future that harnesses the benefits of technology while safeguarding human values, promoting justice, and advancing the well-being of individuals and society as a whole.